Earth and the Solar System

Carol Ballard

Chicago, Illinois

www.heinemannraintree.com
Visit our website to find out
more information about
Heinemann-Raintree books.

To order:
☎ Phone 888-454-2279
🖳 Visit www.heinemannraintree.com
   to browse our catalog and order online.

©2010 Raintree
an imprint of Capstone Global Library, LLC
Chicago, Illinois

Edited by James Nixon
Page layout by sprout.uk.com limited
Original illustrations © Discovery Books Limited 2009
Illustrated by sprout.uk.com limited
Picture research by James Nixon
Originated by Modern Age
Printed and bound in China by South China Printing
  Company Ltd

14 13 12 11 10
10 9 8 7 6 5 4 3 2

Library of Congress Cataloging-in-Publication Data
Ballard, Carol.
   Earth and the solar system / Carol Ballard.
      p. cm. -- (Sci-hi. Earth and space science)
   Includes bibliographical references and index.
   ISBN 978-1-4109-3354-6 (hc)
   -- ISBN 978-1-4109-3364-5 (pb)
   1. Earth--Juvenile literature.
   2. Solar system--Juvenile literature.
   I. Title.
   QB631.4.B35 2010
   523.2--dc22
                         2009013462

Acknowledgments
The author and publishers are grateful to the
following for permission to reproduce copyright
material: Alamy: p. 26 (Peter Arnold, Inc); Getty
Images: p. 38 (Max Dannebaum); NASA: pp. 6, 7
(T.A. Rector and M. Hanna, NOAO/AURA/NSF), 10
(NASA/JPL),18, 19, 23 (NASA/JPL- Caltech/O. Krause,
Steward Observatory), 24, 28, 30 (Magellan Project,
JPL, NASA), 31 (Planetary Photo Journal), 31 (NASA/
JPL/Arizona State University), 33 (NASA/JPL/MSSS), 34
(NASA Headquarters, Greatest Images of NASA), 35
(NASA/JPL), 36 (JPL/STSci), 37 (NASA); Photolibrary:
p. 32 (Colin Anderson); Science Photo Library: pp.8
(Jerry Lodriguss/Science Photo Library), 29 (David
A Hardy/Science Photo Library); Shutterstock: pp. 5
(Jurgen Ziewe), 11 (Roman Sigaev), 13 top left (Andrey
Shadrin), 13 top right (Galina Barskaya), 13 bottom, 15
(Stephen Inglis), 17 (Spectral Design), 47.

Cover photograph of satellite above Earth with
permission of of Getty Images (Erik Simonsen).

We would like to thank content consultant Suzy
Gazlay and text consultant Nancy Harris for their
invaluable help in the preparation of this book.

Contents

Why do some stars explode? Find out on page 23!

Why does the planet Venus get so hot? Find out on page 30!

Some words are shown in bold, **like this**. These words are explained in the glossary. You will find important information and definitions underlined, **<u>like this</u>**.

THE SOLAR SYSTEM

We live on a **planet** we call Earth. This is a rocky ball that goes around the Sun. The Sun is really a **star**, but it looks bigger and brighter than other stars in our sky because it is closer to us. Other planets also go around the Sun, as well as **asteroids, comets, moons, dust, and gases. <u>The Solar System is made up of the Sun and all the things that go around it.</u>**

PLANETS

Some planets are solid and rocky, but others are just giant balls of gas. The eight planets in the Solar System are:

Mercury	Venus	Earth	Mars
Jupiter	Saturn	Uranus	Neptune

Until 2006, Pluto was also called a planet, but now **astronomers** have decided it is too small to be a regular planet. Instead, it is called a **dwarf planet**.

All the planets go around the Sun. Their oval paths are called **orbits**. We say that anything that moves around something else is "orbiting" it. The Sun's **gravity** pulls on the planets and keeps them in their orbits.

SPEED OF ORBIT

In 1605, German mathematician Johannes Kepler described how planets move. He said:

• Planets move faster when they are near the Sun and slower when they are farther away.

• The more distant the planet is from the Sun, the slower its orbit.

We now know he was right.

Earth and other planets of the Solar System move in oval orbits around the Sun.

OLD IDEAS

Ptolemy was a Greek scientist who lived in ancient Egypt nearly 2,000 years ago. He thought the stars were stuck on the inside of a spinning, hollow ball. Earth was fixed at the center of the ball. The Sun and the planets moved in circles around Earth. Ptolemy's ideas were wrong, but people believed them for nearly 1,500 years.

Copernicus, a Polish astronomer who lived about 500 years ago, came up with a new idea, which we now know is true. He said the Sun was at the center of our Solar System. Everything else, including Earth, went around the Sun.

IN THE UNIVERSE . . .

Our Solar System is part of a **galaxy** called the Milky Way. <u>**A galaxy is a cluster of many stars. Each star can have its own solar system**</u>. Our Sun is pretty important to us, but there are hundreds of thousands of other stars in the Milky Way. And the Milky Way is just one galaxy among billions of other galaxies. Together, these make up the **universe**. The universe includes all the stars, galaxies, and empty space. In fact, the universe contains absolutely everything that exists!

This massive cluster of young stars, which is in the Milky Way galaxy, sparkles like jewels!

You can see this spiral-shaped galaxy from Earth using binoculars.

WHERE DO YOU LIVE?

We're all used to writing our address as our house, street, town, state, and country. But you could add more, in this order . . .

Planet Earth, The Solar System, Milky Way Galaxy, The Universe

So next time you want to send a letter home from outer space, you know how to address the envelope!

JOE BRIGHT
I OLD ROAD, ANYTOWN
NEW STATE, USA
PLANET EARTH
THE SOLAR SYSTEM
MILKY WAY GALAXY
THE UNIVERSE

BIG BANG!

Most scientists think the universe began about 13.5 billion years ago, with a huge explosion they call the Big Bang. The Big Bang theory says before the Big Bang happened, absolutely nothing existed. From the Big Bang came all the space, time, **energy**, and **matter** (stuff) in the universe today. At first, the universe was tiny and extremely hot. It gradually cooled and expanded to the size it is now. Scientists are trying to work out whether the universe will keep expanding forever, stay the same size as it is now, or eventually collapse in on itself.

Forces such as gravity developed right after the Big Bang. Then the first **atoms** (tiny units of matter) formed. Some atoms collected together into clouds. These eventually formed stars (or suns) and galaxies.

STAR PATTERNS

What do you see if you look at the sky on a clear night? More stars than you can possibly count! For thousands of years, people have looked at the stars and tried to understand their patterns and movements. Today, scientists have powerful telescopes to look at the sky, but the earliest people just used their eyes.

Early people thought they could see patterns of people and animals in the night sky. We call these groups of stars **constellations**. Eighty-eight constellations are named in Earth's sky.

Which stars you can see depends on three things: where you are on Earth, the time of year, and the time of night. For example, the constellation called the Southern Cross can be seen from the southern hemisphere but not from the northern hemisphere.

This group of stars known as Gemini is named after the twins Castor and Pollux of Greek mythology.

SPACE DISTANCES

On Earth, we measure distances between two places in kilometers or miles. But the distances in space are huge. Astronomers measure them in light-years. One light-year is the distance light can travel in one year—about 9.5 trillion km (nearly 6 trillion miles). The Milky Way galaxy is about 100,000 light-years across. This means that, if you were traveling on a beam of light, it would take you 100,000 years to travel from one side of the Milky Way to the other!

USING STARS

Since ships began sailing long distances across the sea, sailors have used stars to navigate (find their way). The main star they used to help them was Polaris, also called the Pole Star or North Star. An instrument called a **sextant**, which was invented in the 18th century, allowed sailors to work out their exact position. To find how far north or south of the **equator** you are, the sextant measures the angle between the **horizon** and a star. To find out how far east or west you are, it measures the angle between the Moon and a star.

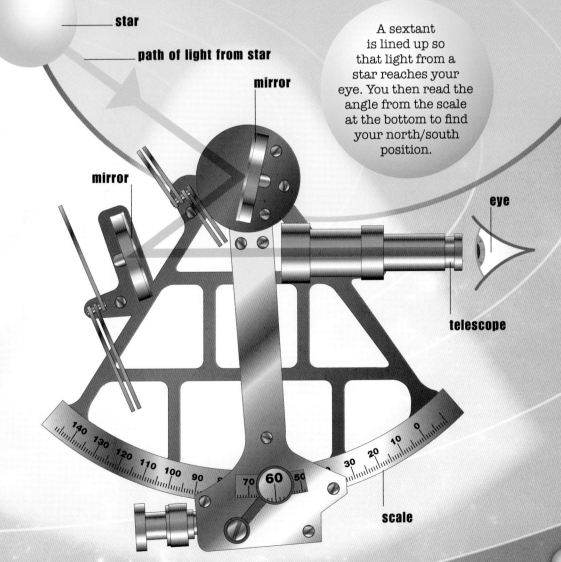

star

path of light from star

mirror

A sextant is lined up so that light from a star reaches your eye. You then read the angle from the scale at the bottom to find your north/south position.

mirror

eye

telescope

scale

PLANET EARTH

Planet Earth is a rocky ball that **orbits** the Sun. At the same time, it spins around nonstop, like a merry-go-round in space. It has everything needed to support life: light, water, heat, and **oxygen.**

WHAT IS EARTH MADE OF?

Earth is not just a solid rocky ball. Instead, it has several layers. At the very center is the **core,** which is made of the metals iron and nickel. Surrounding the core is a layer of liquid rock called the **mantle**. On top of this is a layer of solid rock called the **crust**. The crust is not flat, though—its peaks gives us mountains, and the oceans fill its dips. We live on the surface of the crust, along with plants and animals.

Seen from space, Earth looks like a blue ball. The white patterns are clouds, the green shapes are continents, and the blue is the oceans.

WHAT SURROUNDS EARTH?

Earth itself is surrounded by a layer of gases. This is the air that we breathe. Without it, there would be no life on Earth. This layer of gases is called the **atmosphere** and it stretches many kilometers into space. **The farther away from Earth you go, the thinner and colder the atmosphere becomes**.

IMAGINARY LINES

Have you seen a model of Earth called a globe? A globe is the most accurate map of the world.

EQUATOR – this imaginary line is marked on most globes. It goes right around the middle of Earth, a bit like putting a piece of string around the middle of an orange. The part of Earth above the **equator** is called the northern hemisphere. The part below the equator is the southern hemisphere.

AXIS – this is an imaginary straight line going from the top to the bottom of Earth, through the center. The North Pole is at the top of the **axis,** and the South Pole is at the bottom. If you look at a globe, you'll see that Earth is tipped over a bit. This is the angle that Earth is tilted as it spins around the Sun. The axis isn't quite vertical. This means that the North Pole is not directly above the South Pole.

Have you ever looked closely at a globe? Can you find the equator and the poles? If you spin it, each of the continents will pass in front of you in turn.

North Pole

direction of spin

northern hemisphere

equator

southern hemisphere

axis

South Pole

SPINNING PLANET

It is hard to believe the planet we live on is spinning all the time—yet that really is what is happening! Earth feels perfectly still when we stand on it. We can't feel it or see it moving because Earth is so large. But we can see the effects of its spin, as day turns into night and as the Sun's position changes in the sky.

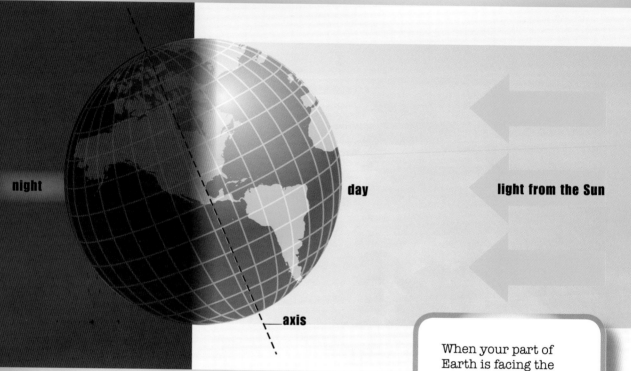

night

day

light from the Sun

axis

DAY AND NIGHT

It takes Earth 24 hours to make one complete turn on its axis. At dawn, the part of Earth you are living on is just turning toward the Sun. The sky becomes lighter as sunlight reaches you.

When your part of Earth is facing the Sun, you have day. When your part of Earth is facing away from the Sun, you have night.

By lunchtime, your part of Earth is facing the Sun, and the daylight is at its brightest. Then Earth starts to turn away from the Sun during the afternoon and evening, and the light slowly fades. By nightfall, your part of Earth is facing away from the Sun. No sunlight can reach you, so it is dark.

The Sun itself does not actually move—it just looks as if it does.

TIME ZONES

As Earth spins, one half will be having day while the other half is having night. Imagine that vertical lines are used to divide Earth into 24 sections. Each section, called a time zone, is one hour ahead of the section that follows it. You can think of it like counting around the segments of a peeled orange. If we did not have different time zones, some places would have daylight at midnight.

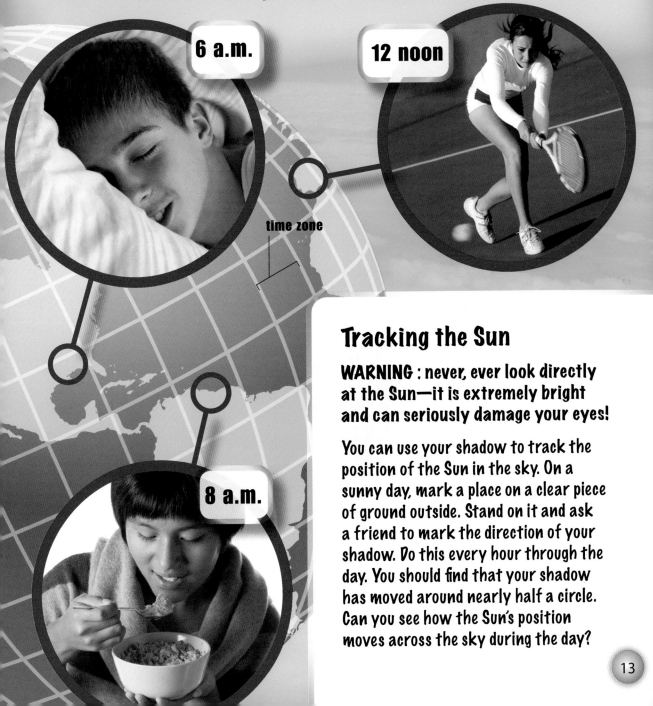

6 a.m.

12 noon

time zone

8 a.m.

Tracking the Sun

WARNING : never, ever look directly at the Sun—it is extremely bright and can seriously damage your eyes!

You can use your shadow to track the position of the Sun in the sky. On a sunny day, mark a place on a clear piece of ground outside. Stand on it and ask a friend to mark the direction of your shadow. Do this every hour through the day. You should find that your shadow has moved around nearly half a circle. Can you see how the Sun's position moves across the sky during the day?

FOUR SEASONS

At the same time as Earth spins on its axis, it also moves in its orbit around the Sun. It takes Earth one year to complete one orbit. The tilt of Earth's axis does not change, so parts of Earth are closer to the Sun at some times than at others.

September 23

autumn equinox (northern hemisphere)
spring equinox (southern hemisphere)

December 22

winter solstice
(northern hemisphere)
summer solstice
(southern hemisphere)

Sun

June 21

summer solstice
(northern hemisphere)
winter solstice
(southern hemisphere)

March 21

spring equinox (northern hemisphere)
autumn equinox (southern hemisphere)

CHANGING SEASONS

Look at the diagram above.

Summer: When your part of Earth is tilted toward the Sun, you have summer. Days are longer, and the weather is hotter.

Autumn: As your part of Earth moves away from the Sun, you have autumn. Days get shorter; nights get longer. The weather becomes cooler.

Winter: When your part of Earth is tilted away from the Sun, you have winter. Days are shorter, and nights are longer. It is cold!

Spring: As your part of Earth moves closer to the Sun, you have spring. Days get longer and nights get shorter. The weather gets warmer.

No seasons?

The part of Earth around the equator stays about the same distance from the Sun all year. This means day length and temperature do not change much through the year.

Solstice and equinox

There are four special times in the year:

Date	Name	What happens?	Why?
March 20 or 21	spring equinox	day and night are equal lengths	North and South Poles are the same distance from the Sun
September 22 or 23	autumn equinox		
June 20 or 21	summer solstice	longest day of the year	northern hemisphere tipped toward the Sun
December 21 or 22	winter solstice	shortest day of the year	northern hemisphere tipped away from Sun

Note: This is written as if you're in the northern hemisphere. If you're in the southern hemisphere, you will need to swap March and September around, and swap June and December. And each time you read "northern hemisphere," replace it with "southern hemisphere."

Amazing fact:

Some ancient cultures used to have special celebrations at the solstices and equinoxes. Some ancient monuments, such as Stonehenge in the United Kingdom and some pyramids in Egypt, are lined up so that the Sun falls on them in a particular way on one or more of these dates.

Satellites

A **satellite** is anything that **orbits** a larger object. The Moon is a satellite of Earth. More than 5,000 artificial (human-made) satellites have been launched since the beginning of the **Space Age.**

Satellites are carried into space by a rocket or the Space Shuttle. Earth's **gravity** holds them in place, stopping them flying off into outer space. Most satellites orbit at between 480 and 36,000 km (300 and 22,500 miles) above the surface of Earth.

The first satellite was launched by the Soviet Union on October 4, 1957. It was called *Sputnik 1*. In 1958, the United States launched its first satellite, *Explorer 1*. Satellites have many uses.

Weather satellites

These are used for weather forecasting and monitoring.

Scientific satellites

This type of satellite carries out exploration. One of the best known is the Hubble Space Telescope, which collects information from deep in space.

Communications satellites

These relay telephone and Internet signals, and television and radio broadcasts.

PARTS OF A SATELLITE

POWER SOURCE: solar cells or fuel cells to charge rechargeable batteries

ONBOARD COMPUTER: controls and monitors everything

METAL BODY: holds satellite together and shields the satellite from extreme temperature changes

ATTITUDE CONTROL SYSTEM: keeps the satellite pointing in the right direction

RADIO SYSTEM: allows communication with controllers on Earth

Military satellites

These are top secret! They collect information, such as enemy positions and movements, and relay it to military bases.

Geostationary satellites

Geostationary satellites stay in the same place above Earth all the time. Their orbit matches the speed of Earth's spin. Most communications satellites are in a geostationary orbit.

Some satellites fly in a polar orbit, passing over the North Pole and the South Pole. This means that they fly over much of Earth's surface. They are ideal for mapping and photography.

Navigational satellites

These pinpoint locations on Earth's surface. For example, a network of 24 satellites allows us to navigate with a global positioning system (GPS). It can tell us exactly where we are and give directions to get to somewhere else.

EARTH'S MOON

Earth's Moon is about one quarter of the size of Earth. Although it is our nearest neighbor in space, it is nearly 400,000 km (250,000 miles) away! Earth's **gravity** keeps it in position. It is the only object in space that humans have visited.

The Moon is the brightest object in our night sky, yet it is not a light source—the Moon does not give out any light of its own! Instead, it is like a huge mirror, reflecting light from the Sun.

The **craters** on the surface of the Moon were made millions of years ago by chunks of space debris smashing into it.

WHAT IS THE MOON LIKE?

The Moon is a ball of rock. The Moon has no water, and its gravity is not strong enough to hold an **atmosphere** in place. This means that nothing can live on the Moon because it has no water and no atmosphere. Harmful rays from the Sun bombard its dusty surface. The dark patches on the Moon's surface are called "seas," but they have never had any water in them. The light patches are called "land" and are covered in hollows called craters. The biggest crater is called Crater Tycho. It is so big you can even see it from Earth.

THE MOON AND TIDES

The Moon's gravity pulls on Earth and everything on it, including the seas and oceans. The pull on the side of Earth closest to the Moon is greater than the pull on the other side. This means that, as Earth spins, different areas of sea are pulled toward the Moon. This causes the movements of the sea that we call **tides**.

Gravity on the Moon is only one sixth as strong as Earth's gravity. This means astronauts only weigh one sixth as much on the Moon as they do on Earth!

THE MOON AND MONTHS

The Moon **orbits** Earth. It takes it 27 ½ days to go around once. This is called a "lunar month." "Lunar" means relating to the Moon. As the Moon orbits Earth, we see its shape changing. The Moon doesn't really change shape, though—it just looks as if it does. This happens because we see different amounts of the lit-up side of the Moon.

AMAZING FACT

Far side: The same side of the Moon always faces Earth. This means that we never see the other side, because it always faces away from Earth.

PROJECT

KEEP A MOON DIARY

Try this activity to track the phases of the Moon.

1 Divide a piece of paper into four rows, each with seven squares. Write today's date at the top of the first box. Then write tomorrow's date in the next box across. Keep adding the next day's date to the next box.

2 At night, look at the Moon. Draw the shape of the Moon that you see in the first box. Color the background black. Tomorrow, look again and draw the shape you see in the next box. If you cannot see the Moon at all, just color the whole box black to show it was a cloudy night.

3 Do this each night until you have filled in all the dates in your Moon diary. Can you see the pattern of the Moon's phases through the month?

MOON PHASES

From new moon to full moon, we see more of the Moon each night for two weeks. This is its "waxing" time. Then from full moon to new moon we see less of the Moon each night for two weeks. This is its "waning" period.

1 Day 1: New Moon
We see none of the lit-up side. The Moon starts its waxing period.

2 Start of week 2:
We see about half of the lit-up side. The Moon is still waxing.

As the Moon orbits Earth, different amounts of the Moon are lit up. How much of the Moon you see depends on its position in relation to the Sun. If the Moon is directly between the Sun and Earth none of the Moon is lit up (new moon) except the side we cannot see.

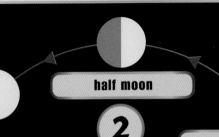

half moon

2

crescent moon

3

full moon

1

new moon

sunlight

4

3 Start of week 3: Full Moon
We see all of the lit-up side. The Moon is waning from now on.

4 Start of week 4: We see about half of the lit-up side. The Moon is waning.

THE SUN

The Sun is a star. It is very important to every living thing on Earth. Without the Sun, nothing would survive.

SUN AND LIFE

The Sun provides all the heat and light on Earth. Plants trap the **energy** in sunlight and make their food. Animals eat the plants and get energy from them. Without the Sun, this could not happen, and everything would die.

Sunlight provides the energy needed for green plants to grow.

WHAT IS A STAR?

Stars are balls of burning gases. Although they might all look very similar to us from Earth, they are really a variety of different sizes, temperatures, and colors. The names tell you what they are like. For example, a red dwarf is a small red star and a blue giant is a large blue star. The color tells you how hot a star is. From coolest to hottest the order is, red—orange—yellow—white—blue.

Life of the Sun

Stars don't stay the same for ever. Their color and size change as they get older. The Sun began as a cloud of gases, called a **nebula**, more than 4 billion years ago. The gases gradually got hotter, a nuclear reaction started, and the gas cloud became a fiery ball—a new star. The Sun will stay like this for about another 4 billion years. Eventually, it will run out of gas. It will collapse inward and then expand before finally fading away.

STAR TYPE	EXAMPLE
red dwarf	Proxima Centauri
yellow dwarf	the Sun
white dwarf	Sirius B
red giant	Betelgeuse

EXPLODING STARS!

Some large stars do not just fade away when they run out of fuel—they end as a spectacular explosion called a **supernova**. The Sun is too small to become a supernova. This picture shows the most recent supernova in the Milky Way.

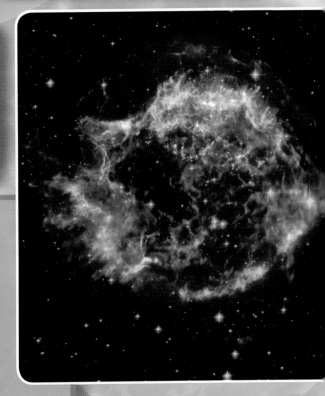

SUN FEATURES

The Sun is about 1.4 million km (870,000 miles) across. You could fit more than 100 Earths into it! It is not solid, but it is made up from two gases: **hydrogen** and **helium**. The gases are kept together because of the Sun's **gravity**.

STRUCTURE OF THE SUN

The Sun has four layers:

1 At the center is the **core**. This is the hottest part, at more than 15 million °C (27 million °F).

2 Around the core is the **radioactive** zone. Materials that are radioactive release invisible high-energy rays that are harmful to humans. Energy produced by the core spreads outward through this layer.

3 Outside this is the **convection** zone, which carries the energy up to the surface.

4 The Sun's surface is called the **photosphere**. It has some special features:

Sunspots are dark patches on the Sun's surface. They are cooler than the rest of the surface.

Prominences are giant loops of gas that leap from the surface. They can move at speeds of around 600 km (370 miles) a second!

Solar flares are violent explosions on the Sun's surface.

In 1973, one of the largest solar prominences ever recorded erupted from the Sun's surface!

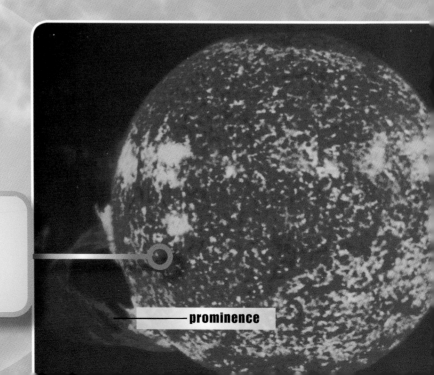

prominence

Solar wind creates amazing light displays in the skies near the North and South Poles.

Energy from the Sun

The Sun is made up from two gases, hydrogen and helium. Hydrogen **atoms** join together in a process called "**nuclear fusion.**" It takes four hydrogen atoms to make one helium atom—and the process releases light energy and heat energy.

Solar wind

Incredibly tiny, invisible **particles** spread out from the Sun in all directions. Together, these particles are called the solar wind. Sometimes, they get trapped at the North or South Poles on Earth. This makes fantastic light displays. When these are seen from areas near the North Pole, they are called the Northern Lights or "aurora borealis." In areas near the South Pole, they are called the Southern Lights or "aurora australis."

ECLIPSE

Eclipses occur when one object in space is in the **shadow of another**. Solar **eclipses** occur when the Moon's shadow falls on Earth. Lunar eclipses occur when Earth's shadow falls on the Moon.

SOLAR ECLIPSE

Warning: Never try to watch a solar eclipse directly—you can seriously and permanently damage your eyes.

During a solar eclipse, the Moon looks like a black disc as it moves slowly across the face of the Sun. When it is exactly between you and the Sun, it is a full black circle. Around its edges is a rim of bright light. A total eclipse is over in just a few minutes.

Not everybody will see a total eclipse. You have to be in exactly the right place on Earth. A partial eclipse occurs when the Moon's shadow does not fall completely on Earth, so part of the Sun can still be seen.

There are several partial solar eclipses every year—but in any given place on Earth, a total solar eclipse happens just once every 360 years!

During a partial solar eclipse, the Moon looks like a black disc in front of the Sun.

HOW A SOLAR ECLIPSE WORKS

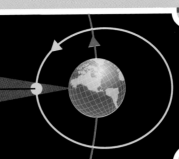

A solar eclipse occurs when the Moon comes between the Sun and Earth. The Moon's shadow falls on Earth.

LUNAR ECLIPSE

Lunar eclipses can occur only at full moon. During a lunar eclipse, Earth passes between the Sun and the Moon. This blocks the Sun's light. You can see Earth's shadow move slowly across the surface of the Moon.

Lunar eclipses last for much longer than solar eclipses, often for one or more hours. Everyone on the side of Earth that is in night can see them. You can watch them safely without needing any eye protection.

STRANGE BUT TRUE

Ancient cultures had legends and myths to explain eclipses. In ancient China, for example, some people thought an eclipse occurred because a dragon was eating the Sun. They banged gongs and drums to scare the dragon away!

HOW A LUNAR ECLIPSE WORKS

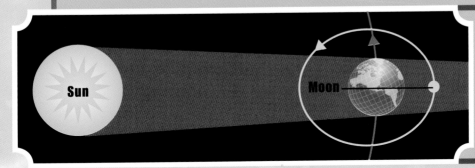

A lunar eclipse occurs when Earth comes between the Sun and the Moon. Earth's shadow falls on the Moon.

Mercury, Venus, and Mars

MERCURY

Mercury is the nearest **planet** to the Sun, and it is the smallest planet in the Solar System. It is dry and dusty, and its surface is covered in **craters**. Mercury has no moons.

VERY HOT—OR VERY COLD?

Mercury is neither the hottest nor the coldest planet, but it does have the widest range of temperatures. Days on Mercury can be as hot as 450 °C (840 °F), while the night temperature can be as low as -183 °C (-297 °F). On Earth, the **atmosphere** provides protection from the heat of the Sun during the day and traps heat in at night. Mercury's atmosphere is very thin. It cannot prevent the temperature extremes.

Caloris Basin

The Caloris Basin is one of the biggest craters in the Solar System. It is 1,300 km (800 miles) across. That's more than the distance from one end of California to the other! The Caloris Basin was formed when Mercury collided with an **asteroid** (huge space rock). The impact was so enormous that scientists think **shock waves** from it may have made the big rocky ridges on the opposite side of the planet.

The circles on the surface of Mercury are craters made when asteroids crashed into the planet!

28

Two sunrises?

Mercury does not **orbit** the Sun at a steady speed—it speeds up and slows down. But it keeps spinning at the same speed all the time. This makes some strange things happen. Sometimes, the sun rises very slowly, stops, and then goes back down and sets. Then it stops, rises again, and keeps on going until the next "year."

The fastest planet

Mercury orbits the Sun more quickly than any other planet. It takes just 88 days to go around it once.

Naming Mercury

Mercury was the "messenger" of the gods in ancient Rome. The Romans gave the planet its name because it moved so quickly across the night sky. Mercury's symbol (right) is a circle above a small cross, with a half-circle on top. It represents the messenger's helmet and staff.

The surface of Mercury is dry—and there is no atmosphere to protect it from the heat of the Sun during the day.

VENUS

Venus is the second planet from the Sun. It is Earth's nearest neighbor—but you really wouldn't want to visit it. You wouldn't be able to breathe, and the **pressure** of the atmosphere is so great you'd be crushed to death pretty quickly! Its surface is covered in craters and volcanoes. Venus has no moons.

GREENHOUSE EFFECT

The atmosphere on Venus is really thick and nasty, and it is mainly carbon dioxide gas. Very thick clouds, made of **sulfuric acid**, cover the whole planet. The heavy atmosphere acts like a giant blanket in the sky. It traps the heat from the Sun, so the planet gets really hot. It's farther from the Sun than Mercury, so you'd expect it to be cooler—but in fact it's hotter, and can reach an amazing 464 °C (867 °F).

Slow spinner

Venus takes only 225 days to orbit the Sun, but it takes Venus 243 Earth days to spin once on its axis. This means that one day on Venus lasts longer than one year!

"Morning Star" and "Evening Star"

Venus can be seen from Earth at sunrise and sunset as well as at night. It shines brightly and looks like a **star**—and so it is often called the "Morning Star" and the "Evening Star."

MARS

Mars is the fourth planet from the Sun. It is about 229 million km (142 million miles) from the Sun and is about half the size of Earth.

THE SURFACE OF MARS

Mars is a rocky planet, and it looks red from space. This is because the soil contains a lot of iron oxide—the red **chemical** we know as rust. Because of this, it is often called the Red Planet. Mars has many volcanoes, but none are active. Two amazing surface features are:

- A giant canyon system of gorges (steep valleys) slices through the rocks around the **equator**. It is more than 3,000 km (1,850 miles) long.

- The biggest volcano in the Solar System. It is more than 24 km (15 miles) high and 600 km (375 miles) across. It has been named Olympus Mons. The volcano covers an area almost the size of the state of Arizona.

This photograph shows part of the Grand Canyon on Mars. The canyon averages over 160 km (100 miles) in width and can be up to 6.5 km (4 miles) deep.

NASA's Hubble Space Telescope took this photo of Mars. The ring shape near the middle is Olympus Mons, one of the biggest volcanoes in the Solar System.

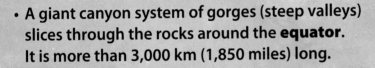

Olympus Mons

LIFE ON MARS?

Are science fiction films telling the truth? Could Martians be real? Might there be green monsters living on Mars? We know that living things like the plants and animals on Earth could not live on Mars. But might some other forms of life live there?

A living thing on Mars would have three major problems. The temperature, the air, and the water are far from ideal.

WARMTH ON MARS?

The **planet** is farther from the Sun than Earth, so it is colder. Winter nights can be bitterly cold, dropping to as low as -140 °C (-220 °F). Anything living on Mars would have to be able to survive the cold!

Little green men?

If Martians do exist, they will not look like the little green monsters of science fiction. Instead, scientists think that, if there are any living organisms on Mars, they are likely to be tiny, similar to the **bacteria** found on Earth.

BREATHING ON MARS?

The atmosphere on Mars is mainly carbon dioxide, so humans would not be able to breathe there. But it might suit a life form that used carbon dioxide gas.

Scientists have detected the gas **methane** on Mars. This could be produced by **chemical reactions** in the rocks. But on Earth, some methane is also produced by living things. It is possible that the methane on Mars was produced by tiny living things similar to bacteria.

WATER ON MARS?

Water is essential for life as we know it. Mars has frozen ice caps at its poles, similar to those on Earth. But . . . the ice is not pure frozen water! Instead, it is mainly frozen carbon dioxide, mixed with just a little water.

Some frozen water has been found underground on Mars. Scientists think they may also find liquid water there, too.

Could the layers in the rocks be evidence that there was once life on Mars?

Clues in the rocks

The rocks on Mars suggest that, at one time, there may have been lots of water there. Channels in the surface rocks of Mars might be dried-up riverbeds.

Some rocks are striped, with uneven layers. These look like Earth's sandstone and limestone that formed on the beds of oceans and rivers millions of years ago. So it is possible that these striped Martian rocks also formed underwater.

GAS GIANTS

The four **planets** beyond Mars are Jupiter, Saturn, Uranus, and Neptune. These are not made of rock. Instead, they are huge balls of gas with just a tiny central rocky **core**. This means that they have no real surface on which a spacecraft could land. They are known as the gas giants.

JUPITER

Jupiter really is a giant planet. At an amazing 143,000 km (nearly 90,000 miles) across, it is the biggest planet in the Solar System. Its clouds are full of colors because they contain a complex mixture of gases that **react** with each other.

GREAT RED SPOT

Jupiter's giant red spot is so big it can be seen even from Earth. It is a huge, 300-year-old thunderstorm!

JUPITER'S RINGS

Jupiter has many rings, although they can be seen only faintly from Earth. They are made from fragments of rock, which scientists think are probably the result of ancient **meteor** collisions with Jupiter's moons.

JUPITER'S MOONS

At least 63 moons **orbit** Jupiter, and there may be many more tiny ones! The four main moons are called Io, Europa, Ganymede, and Callisto.

Jupiter is at the top of this photo, with three of its moons: Europa, Ganymede, and Callisto.

The international Cassini-Huygens mission sent the Cassini Orbiter to explore Saturn's rings. It sent back amazing photos like this to scientists on Earth.

SATURN

Saturn is smaller than Jupiter, but bigger than all the other planets in the Solar System. Its gas clouds are very similar to Jupiter's, but they are not as colorful.

SATURN'S RINGS

Saturn has bands of rings that are made up from millions of separate chunks of rock, dust, and ice that orbit the planet. The rings are believed to be pieces of **comets** and **asteroids** that broke up before they reached the planet. Shattered moons may also make up part of Saturn's rings.

AMAZING FACT

Although Saturn is enormous, it is very light for its size. In fact, it's so light that it would float on water!

Most planets spin with their poles at top and bottom—but Uranus spins on its side! Its rings follow this pattern, too.

URANUS

The clouds that swirl around Uranus' core of rocks and ice are made up mainly from **methane**, **hydrogen**, and **helium**. These gases make it look a greenish-blue color. It has faint rings and more are being discovered. Uranus has at least 27 moons, the largest ones being called Oberon, Titania, Umbriel, Ariel, and Miranda. These names are all characters from plays by William Shakespeare.

DAY AND NIGHT ON URANUS

Days and nights are really odd on Uranus. Instead of spinning around and around with its poles at the top and bottom, Uranus spins on its side, rolling around its poles. It spends half its orbit with one pole facing the Sun and half with the other pole facing the Sun. This means that a day and a night together take the same time as one orbit—84 years! (In case you haven't worked it out, it would ALWAYS be your birthday on Uranus.) There is only a single day and night every year.

Neptune

Neptune's blue color comes from its clouds of hydrogen, helium, and methane gas. It has violent storms and strong, fast winds that can reach speeds of 2,000 kph (more than 1,200 mph). Like the other gas giants, Neptune also has a system of rings. Neptune is warmer than you would expect, given that it is so far from the Sun. This makes scientists think it might have its own internal heat source.

Day and night on Neptune

At just over 16 hours, a day on Neptune is about two-thirds of an Earth day. You wouldn't live a year on Neptune, though, as one Neptune year lasts for nearly 165 Earth years!

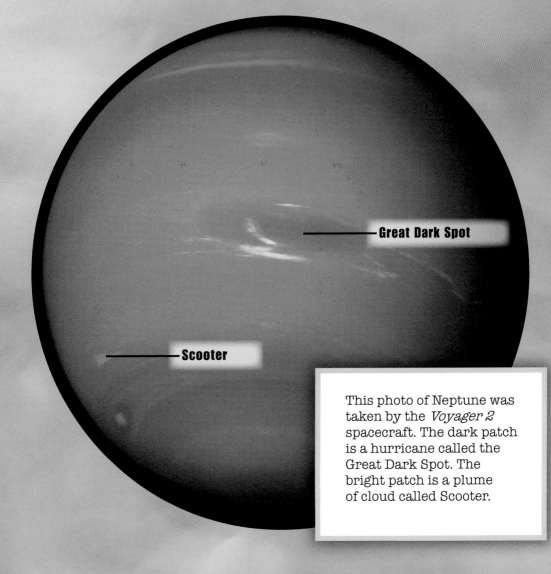

Great Dark Spot

Scooter

This photo of Neptune was taken by the *Voyager 2* spacecraft. The dark patch is a hurricane called the Great Dark Spot. The bright patch is a plume of cloud called Scooter.

ASTEROIDS AND COMETS

In addition to **planets** and their moons, other objects also **orbit the Sun. These** include **asteroids** and **comets.**

ASTEROIDS

<u>Asteroids are lumps of rock in space left behind when the planets and moons first formed</u>. Most are found in a ring known as the Main Belt between Mars and Jupiter. Another ring of asteroids, the Kuiper Belt, is farther away from the Sun, beyond Neptune.

NEAR-EARTH ASTEROIDS

Earth's surface has about 160 **craters** made when large asteroids crashed into Earth. Asteroids that enter Earth's **atmosphere** are known as **"meteors."** It is very rare for meteors to hit land. Most meteors burn up in the atmosphere. They can be seen in the sky as shooting stars.

A large asteroid can smash into a planet at great speed, causing vast disruption and damage!

Dinosaur Destruction?

The Chicxulub Crater in Mexico was made when a huge **meteorite** hit Earth about 65 million years ago. Dust thrown into the atmosphere blocked the heat and light from the Sun for a long time. Many living things died. Some scientists think that the after-effects also wiped out the dinosaurs!

COMETS

Comets are like giant space snowballs! They are lumps of ice and dust that together make up a huge cloud. This is called the Oort Cloud, and it surrounds the Solar System.

SEEING COMETS

You cannot see comets from Earth because they are too small and too far away. Sometimes, though, a comet breaks away from the Oort Cloud and travels toward the Sun. It gets warmer as it nears the Sun, and the ice turns to gas. This leaves a trail of light that we can see in the sky.

Comets streak across space leaving a trail of light behind them.

Halley's Comet

Halley's Comet has been observed from Earth for centuries. Edmond Halley, a British scientist who lived about 300 years ago, worked out that it appears in Earth's skies roughly every 75 or 76 years. The comet was named after him. Halley's Comet was last seen in 1986, and it should reappear in the middle of 2061—look out for it!

Discovery

12 TO 14 BILLION YEARS AGO
The **universe** begins with the huge explosion called the Big Bang!

10 BILLION YEARS AGO
Milky Way forms

4.5 BILLION YEARS AGO
The Sun and **planets** of the Solar System begin to form

1223 BCE
Babylonian **astronomers** record a solar **eclipse** for the first time

1543 CE
Copernicus suggests the Sun is at the center of the Solar System and that all the planets go around the Sun

1605 CE
Johannes Kepler shows that planets move in oval-shaped (elliptical) **orbits**. He also shows that planets move faster when they are near the Sun and slower when they are farther away, and that the more distant the planet from the Sun, the slower its orbit.

1664 CE
Robert Hooke discovers Jupiter's Great Red Spot

Timeline

1781 CE

William Herschel discovers Uranus

1846

Johann Galle discovers Neptune

1927

Big Bang theory first suggested

1930

Clyde Tombaugh discovers Pluto

1957

First **satellite**, *Sputnik I*, launches

1959

Russian spacecraft *Luna II* lands on the Moon

1976

Spacecraft *Viking I* lands on Mars

1979 TO TODAY

Spacecrafts *Voyager 1* and *2* fly past Jupiter, past Saturn and Uranus, and eventually, in 1989, past Neptune. They are still going. *Voyager 1* is now the most distant human-made object in space.

SUMMARY QUIZ

How much did you learn reading this book? Take this quiz and find out. How many out of ten can you get right?

1 One of Jupiter's moons is called:

a) Oberon

b) Io

c) Phobos

d) Pluto

2 The Sun is made of **hydrogen** and:

a) methane

b) oxygen

c) carbon dioxide

d) helium

3 The **planet** nearest to the Sun is:

a) Mercury

b) Mars

c) Neptune

d) Venus

4 The Milky Way is a:

a) solar system

b) planet

c) star

d) galaxy

5 The imaginary line joining the North and South Pole of a planet is called its:

a) **equator** b) **axis**

c) spin line d) slant

6 The Moon is held in its orbit around Earth by:

a) **tides**

b) the Sun

c) itself

d) Earth's **gravity**

7 From coldest to hottest, the order of stars' colors is:

a) red—orange—yellow—white—blue

b) blue—white—yellow—orange—red

c) white—yellow—orange—red—blue

8 Approximately how many years ago was the Big Bang?

a) 5 million

b) 5 billion

c) 13.5 million

d) 18 billion

9 A solar **eclipse** occurs when:

a) Earth's shadow falls on the Sun

b) the Sun moves between Earth and the Moon

c) the Moon's shadow falls on Earth

10 Mars looks red because its soil contains:

a) carbon

b) **hydrogen**

c) rust

d) ice

Answers on page 47

Glossary

asteroid small rocky object in space

astronomer scientist who studies stars, planets, and other objects in space

atmosphere layer of gases that surrounds a planet or moon

atom smallest part of an element that can exist on its own

axis imaginary line through the center of Earth joining the North Pole and the South Pole

bacteria very tiny organisms

chemical particular type of substance made up of one type of molecule

chemical reaction process that involves a change in the structure of the molecules in a substance

comet chunk of ice and dust that orbits the Sun. Comets have a trail of gas and dust pointing away from the Sun.

constellation cluster of stars that make an imaginary picture

convection process by which heat travels through gases and liquids

core central part of an object, such as a planet or star

crater wide hole in the ground caused by something hitting it

crust outer layer of Earth

dwarf planet space object like a planet but smaller

eclipse event that happens when one space object is in the shadow of another

energy power to do something or make something happen

equator imaginary line around the middle of Earth, dividing the top half from the bottom half

equinox the time when North and South Poles are the same distance from the Sun

fuel cell cell that uses chemical reactions to produce an electric current

galaxy huge number of stars and their solar systems

geostationary staying above the same point on Earth's surface

gravity force that pulls objects together

helium very light gas. It is produced by stars.

horizon distant line where the sky seems to touch the land or sea

hydrogen colorless gas. It is the lightest and commonest element in the universe.

light-year distance light can travel in one year

mantle part of Earth that lies between the crust and the core

matter another word for material or substance

meteor lump of rock that travels through a planet's atmosphere. It can often be seen as a shooting star (streak of light).

meteorite chunk of rock that hits the surface of a planet or moon

methane colorless, odorless gas

nebula huge cloud of dust and gas in outer space

nuclear fusion nuclear reaction in which atoms join together and release energy

orbit movement of one object around another

oxygen colorless and odorless gas essential for life as we know it

particles small parts of something

photosphere outer layer of the Sun or another star

planet huge ball of rock or gas that orbits a star

pressure force that is produced by pushing on something

prominence giant loop of gas that leaps from the Sun's surface

radioactive giving off harmful energy rays

react undergo a chemical or physical change as a result of interaction with another substance

satellite space object that orbits another object in space

sextant navigation aid that uses the stars to work out location

shock waves waves of energy sent out when, for example, rocks are shifted due to an earthquake

solar cell device that converts sunlight directly into electricity

solar flare violent explosion on the Sun's surface

solar system star and everything that orbits it

solstice time when one hemisphere is at its closest to, or farthest from, the Sun

Space Age era since 1957 when exploration of space became possible with launched spacecraft

star ball of hot, burning gases that gives off light and heat energy

sulfuric acid very strong acid containing the chemical element sulfur

sunspot dark patch on the Sun's surface

supernova explosion of an old, large star

tides regular changes in the level of the sea on the shore, caused by the pull of the Moon's gravity

universe space and everything that exists

Find Out More

Books

Aguilar, David, *Planets, Stars, and Galaxies: A Visual Encyclopedia of Our Universe*. Des Moines, IA: National Geographic Society, 2007.

Glass, Susan, *The Solar System, (Reading Essentials in Science series)*. Logan, IA: Perfection Learning, 2005.

Goldsmith, Mike, *Solar System*. New York: Kingfisher, 2006.

Ridpath, Gregory, *DK Handbook: Stars and Planets*. New York: DK Publishing, 2000.

Royston, Angela, *Alien Neighbors?: The Solar System*. Chicago: Heinemann, 2005.

Scott, Carole, and Gorton, Steve, *Space Exploration (Eyewitness Books series)*. New York: DK Publishing, 2004.

Silverstein, Alvin; Silverstein, Virginia B.; and Silverstein Nunn, Laura, *Universe, (Science Concepts series)*. New York: Lerner, 2003.

Vogt, Ian, *Our Universe (series)*. Chicago: Heinemann, 2003.

Websites

http://solarsystem.nasa.gov/kids
Website of NASA, United States, with masses of information, slideshows, and images on space

http://hubblesite.org/gallery
Gallery of images from the Hubble Space Telescope

http://www.kidsastronomy.com
Astronomy site specially designed for children and teenagers, with information and games

http://www.cosmos4kids.com/files/solsyst_intro.html
Astronomy site with a lot of information as well as stunning images, activities, and slideshows

http://www.astronomy.com (click on "astronomy for kids" on menu)
Website with information, animations, and ideas for activities and projects

Quiz answers

Q1: b, Q2: d, Q3: a, Q4: d, Q5: b, Q6: d, Q7: a, Q8: d, Q9: c, Q10: c

Index